Unity in Marriage

Becoming A Unified Force

Jennifer Peikert

XULON PRESS

Xulon Press
2301 Lucien Way #415
Maitland, FL 32751
407.339.4217
www.xulonpress.com

© 2023 by Jennifer Peikert

All rights reserved solely by the author. The author guarantees all contents are original and do not infringe upon the legal rights of any other person or work. No part of this book may be reproduced in any form without the permission of the author.

Due to the changing nature of the Internet, if there are any web addresses, links, or URLs included in this manuscript, these may have been altered and may no longer be accessible. The views and opinions shared in this book belong solely to the author and do not necessarily reflect those of the publisher. The publisher therefore disclaims responsibility for the views or opinions expressed within the work.

Unless otherwise indicated, Scripture quotations taken from the Amplified Bible (AMP). Copyright © 2015 by The Lockman Foundation. Used by permission. All rights reserved. Scripture quotations taken from The Message (MSG). Copyright © 1993, 1994, 1995, 1996, 2000, 2001, 2002. Used by permission of NavPress Publishing Group. Used by permission. All rights reserved. Scripture quotations taken from the New King James Version (NKJV). Copyright © 1982 by Thomas Nelson, Inc. Used by permission. All rights reserved. Scripture quotations taken from the Holy Bible, New International Version (NIV). Copyright © 1973, 1978, 1984, 2011 by Biblica, Inc.™. Used by permission. All rights reserved.

Paperback ISBN-13: 978-1-66288-221-0
Ebook ISBN-13: 978-1-66288-222-7

DEDICATION

I would like to first dedicate this book to God. Thank you, God, for loving me and for enabling me to write this book. Thank you for helping my husband, Jay, and myself, to have the marriage of our dreams.

I would also like to dedicate this book to marriages all over the world. May the truths in the Word of God, and the truths in the pages of this book, forever impact your lives and your marriages.

CONTENT

Foreword..ix
Acknowledgement.......................................xi
Introduction...xiii

Chapter 1: Unity, what does it Mean?...................1
Chapter 2: Why is Unity Important?....................13
Chapter 3: Why is Unity so Important in Marriage?....13
Chapter 4: God's Plan for Marriage....................20
Chapter 5: The Role of the Husband....................29
Chapter 6: The Role of the Wife.......................36
Chapter 7: The Role of God in Marriage................44
Chapter 8: Where do we go from Here? -
           United for Purpose.........................52
Chapter 9: Friendship in Marriage.....................62
Chapter 10: Onward and Upward.........................70

Prayer for Marriages..................................75
About the Author......................................77
Other Books by Jennifer Peikert.......................77

FOREWORD

Marriage is the most sacred institution known to man.

*P*aul says, in Ephesians 5:31-32, that this profound mystery of two people – a groom and a bride – becoming one, isn't only speaking about a marriage covenant between people, but about the covenant between Christ (the Bridegroom) and the Church (the Bride). He likens our earthly marriage unity to the unity between Christ and the Church. Paul is letting us know about the power present when two people become one.

We have known Jennifer and her husband, Jay, for years. We are their pastors and have watched them closely. They minister in our "Healing Rooms," an inner healing ministry at our church. We trust them implicitly, and my husband and I have marveled at their unity, especially in marriage, ministry, and occupation. This couple has been married almost as long as my husband and I. We both know that being in ministry together requires a lot of love and patience. When you're around another person who perhaps is different than you and has a different expression than you, then you should be learning quite a bit about yourself. Jay and Jennifer are not only ministry partners, but business partners as well. As owners of a family business, they have discovered keys to working together and ministering together. Jennifer shares her profound insight into the keys of unity, and the power it expresses.

The enemy wants nothing more than to destroy the institution that Christ likens to His marriage with the Church. With divorce statistics at almost forty-five percent, disunity is soaring out of control. This book offers great solutions to complicated issues. God clearly defines what marriage is and our various roles within our marriages. Jennifer beautifully outlines these in her book. As Christians, we should use The Word (The Bible) as a blueprint or map to follow for success. This author does a great job outlining the scriptural definitions of unity between husband and wife, describing the kind of power that a unified marriage has.

Many couples are now choosing to not marry because of the high divorce rate. This is not the will of our Father for the generations. His desire is for the family unit to be like the family unit He describes in His Word. I believe that this book, along with the biblical teachings in The Word, will give direction to those who are married, who want to be married, or who are trying marriage again. As a believer in the marriage covenant, I whole-heartedly recommend this book.

Robin Bohlin,
Administrative Pastor of Fullness in Christ Church,
Fort Worth, Texas, and
happily married to Jonas Bohlin
for forty-three wonderful years!

ACKNOWLEDGEMENT

I want to thank God for choosing me to write this book, for equipping me, and helping me write every word. Thank you for being my Savior and loving me unconditionally.

I want to thank my husband, Jay, for loving Jesus the way you do. Thank you for loving me, believing in me, and supporting me. You truly are incredible. Thank you for putting God first in your life, and surrendering your life to Him. I love you with all that is in me.

I want to thank my amazing "mother-in-love," Martha Peikert, for all she does for me. Thank you for typing this manuscript and all the hours it has taken to type and edit. You are incredible and I love you dearly. I am beyond blessed to have you for my *mom*.

I want to thank Xulon Press and all the staff that helped get this book into the hands of the world. You are all wonderful to work with.

Thank you to my sons and daughters-in-love for all you do for me and for your love.

Thank you to our pastors, Jonas and Robin Bohlin, for all of your love and support and for believing in the call that God has on both Jay's life and mine. We love you very much.

Thank you to all of our church family and our wonderful and amazing friends (you know who you are). Your love, support, and prayers are greatly appreciated and needed. I love each of you so much.

Thank you to Carlton and Deborah Edwards and Declaration Ministries for seeing the things God has put in us, and for helping pull them out of us. We treasure our friendship and love you dearly.

INTRODUCTION

My prayer is that as you read the pages of this book, you will understand what unity in marriage is, and how to walk in it, so that your marriage will be unified and you will walk in unity and power with your spouse. God has so much in store for you and your spouse. The enemy tries to keep marriages divided because even he knows about the power a united couple has. He knows what will happen when you unite with your spouse for God's divine purposes for your lives and your marriage, and he doesn't want it.

The pages of this book are full of scripture, wisdom, and personal experiences. As you delve into this book, do so with an open mind and heart, and allow God to give you revelation from Heaven for your own lives and marriages. May you receive everything and more as you read this book.

There is so much power when a husband and wife come into unity, both with each other and with God. You will learn what unity means, why it is important, how important friendship is in a marriage, and the roles the wife and husband play in unity.

God had me write this book for His divine purpose. In a time where divorce is so high and so easily obtained, this truth is vital. God wants marriage to be for life, not only when it is easy and everything is good, not only for a time, until something better is available. It is for *life*. God has a tremendous plan for you, your spouse, and your marriage. If you haven't already, it is time to learn and get on this journey with God. It is time for you, your spouse, and your marriage to be *all* God desires it to be. Let's start this journey and step into the *fullness* of all God has for you.

Chapter 1

UNITY: WHAT DOES IT MEAN?

*I*n this chapter, we will learn what unity is all about, what it really means, and prayerfully, we will get this meaning deep in our hearts and in our understanding as we begin this book.

Let's take time to look up the definition of unity through several different tools:

Webster's Dictionary defines <u>unity</u> as, "the state of being one; being united; oneness; harmony; agreement; concord; unification; a group or body formed by this; an arrangement of parts that will produce a single harmonious effect."

<u>Unity</u> in *Unger's Bible Dictionary* is defined as, "to signify a oneness of sentiment, affection or behavior, such as should exist among the people of God."

<u>Unity</u> in *Nelson's Super Value Series Illustrated Dictionary of the Bible* is defined as: "oneness, harmony, agreement."

Unity was apparent on the day of Pentecost, when the believers "were all with one accord in one place," (Acts 2:1). The church is united in a fellowship of faith, hope, and love that binds believers together (Eph. 4: 3,13).

So, what is unity? It is a harmony, a oneness, an agreement of *two or more*. Unity is an important factor among the church, the home, and in marriage. Unity binds two or more together and it signifies a oneness. Where there is unity, there is strength.

Acts 2: 1-2 (NKJV) in The Woman's Study Bible states:

> *When the Day of Pentecost had fully come they were all with one accord in one place. Suddenly there came a sound from Heaven, as of a mighty rushing wind, and it filled the whole house where they were sitting.*

Wow, see what happens when there is unity – one accord. There is power in unity.

Psalm 133:1 says, *"How good and pleasant it is when brothers live together in unity."* Unity is a great and powerful thing. It is a *God* thing, and extremely important in our lives.

To me, unity produces strength. Unity causes us to be fortified. Where there is unity, there is peace.

> Ephesians 4:3 and 13 say, *"make every effort to keep the unity of the Spirit through the bond of peace.* [13] *until we all reach unity in the faith and in the knowledge of the Son of God and become*

> *mature, attaining to the whole measure of the fullness of Christ."*

The Word of God tells us in this scripture to make every effort to keep the unity of the Spirit. To keep the unity of the Spirit means to remain in agreement, to remain in oneness of the Spirit.

> Romans 15:5 says, *"May the God who gives endurance and encouragement give you a spirit of unity among yourselves as you follow Christ Jesus."*

So, according to this, God can give us a Spirit of unity. We need to ask God to help us remain in unity and to keep us in a spirit of unity.

> John 27: 22–23 reads, *"I have given them the glory that You gave Me that they may be one; I in them and You in Me. May they be brought to complete unity to let the world know that You sent Me and have loved them even as You have loved Me."*

This scripture is actually Jesus talking. Jesus prayed that we be brought to unity. You can see the importance of unity. It is <u>very</u> important.

Do you remember the statement, "United we stand, divided we fall?" It is very true.

If you have a group of people united with one another on an issue, more than likely, they will win that issue because they are united with one another, and they will not move or be persuaded to be any different. Two or more people in agreement on an issue will generally not be persuaded to change their mind. Yet, if the same two or more people are *not* in agreement, one could definitely be persuaded to change. Unity stands strong. Unity is not easily moved.

Where there is unity, there is peace. You will not find division or unrest in unity.

If unity were not important, Jesus would not have spoken about it, nor would it be mentioned in the Bible.

When unity is present in a church service – *wow* – it is powerful: One body of believers in unity glorifying God. I can almost guarantee the Spirit of God will move in that place and among the people. You can certainly tell the difference in a service where the praise and worship team are in complete unity, and one where they are not. When a worship team is in unity, everything flows wonderfully and sounds tremendous. But, if they are not in unity, it does not flow well, and at times, will not sound very good.

Where there is unity, there is joy. In the midst of unity, there is power. In the center of unity, there is strength. Oh, how important unity is. It is *especially* important between a husband and wife. It is also important to have unity in your household. We will get more into that later in the book.

Unity is a oneness among people. Unity produces peace. Unity produces strength. When unity is not present, there are cracks that will allow the enemy to enter. But, when there is unity, it seals those cracks.

The Lord keeps speaking to me, and says, "A unified force." A unified force is something to be reckoned with. When we stand as a unified force, the devil better watch out.

To <u>unify</u> means, "to make into a *unit*; cause to become one; consolidate; unite," (*Webster's Dictionary*).

"Force," in Webster's Dictionary, means, "strength; energy; power; any group of people organized for some activity; to take by force." So, what is God saying by a "unified force?" He wants His people to be in agreement, to be one in unity. He wants His people to be unified in energy and power to overcome the devil, and to fulfill our purpose here on earth. God has a purpose for each and every one of us, individually, and as a group.

We were put on this earth to fulfill His plan. We are a part of the army of God, and God wants that army to be unified – to walk in unity.

God never wanted churches and people to divide. He wants us to walk in unity to fulfill His purpose here on earth.

You were not put on this earth only to survive. You were put on this earth to **thrive**. You were put on this earth to walk in unity with others and be that "unified force."

As I am writing this, the Lord is giving me a vision of a unified force – one locked hand-in-hand. That force cannot be broken; it is solid. The enemy cannot break through. Next, He gave me a vision of a force not unified, not locked hand-in-hand. The enemy can break through such a force because there is a weakness where there is not unity. Where there is unity, there is strength and energy. There is a force to be reckoned with where there is unity.

The enemy knows what will happen when there is unity. That is why he tries to keep things stirred up, and keep strife among people.

Unity means: peace, joy, power, oneness, strength, agreement, and fortification. It is a force to be reckoned with.

Remember these things as you begin digging deeper into the meaning of unity, and allow the Lord to speak to you as you read this book.

Let's move on to the next chapter which delves more into the importance of unity.

Chapter 2

WHY IS UNITY IMPORTANT?

Unity is important because where there is unity, there is strength, peace, power, energy, and happiness. I have been in situations where there was not unity and you could feel the unrest and the discord.

As Christian individuals, we should be so unified (one) with Jesus that people can't tell us apart. When we align ourselves in agreement with Jesus, there is no stopping us.

One of the devil's tools is strife. He wants to keep us at odds with each other, instead of in unity with each other, because he knows what will happen when we come into unity with each other. He knows what will happen to him and his plans once we become that unified force. If a home is not in unity, the Word says it will not stand. So we need to do the best we can to have unity in our homes.

> Matthew 12:25 says, *"Jesus knew their thoughts and said to them, 'Every kingdom divided against itself will be ruined and every city or household divided against itself will not stand.'"*

This is Jesus talking. There is strength in unity. There is no greater power than when a husband and wife are in unity. There is strength, power, and energy in unity.

A house divided against itself will not stand; so, the opposite would be true of a house in unity – it **will** stand. Unity will prevail. A unified force is a strong and powerful force, one not to be broken or defeated.

Think about a football team for a minute. If you have a football team that is unified and plays in unity, their plays will go smooth and the team will flow together. And, more than likely, they will win.

It is time, we as believers, get in unity and charge the devil instead of him charging us because we are divided and weak when not standing as a complete body. A unified force and people in unity are not a force easily torn down. It is not a force easily broken through.

The Church has allowed the devil to attack and steal from them long enough. It is time for the Church to rise up, join forces, be in unity, and overcome the enemy.

God is calling us to unity, to be in unity, and fulfill His plan for the church in these last days. He is calling us to His original plan for the church. His plan was not for us to divide, but to unite as one. The devil is defeated; Jesus defeated him permanently. God is calling us, as a body of believers, to take our position and be that united force against the enemy.

All the different beliefs and religions are not God's plan. He planned for us to be in unity, and be a unified force. We were put on this earth to fulfill His desires and purposes, not to be at odds and divided. Division is the devil's plan; unity is God's plan and God's way. When people are not united, peace does not exist; strife does. Where there is division, there is strife. Where there is strife, there is division. God wants us to live in peace, not division.

> Remember Matthew 12:25: *"Jesus knew their thoughts and said to them: 'Every kingdom divided against itself will be ruined and every city or household divided against itself will not stand.'"*

We must be in unity with our spouse. Unity is from the Lord, but division is from the enemy (Satan). I am not going to choose the way of the enemy, and be in division. I will choose unity.

Mark 3:25 says, *"If a house is divided against itself, that house cannot stand."* Jesus is saying this. Do you see the importance of staying in unity? The Word says that when a house is divided, it will not, and *cannot* stand.

How many of you have ever been in an argument with your spouse where you could not stand the strife it brought? How many of you have argued with your spouse until bedtime, and you couldn't go to sleep because you had absolutely no peace? How many of you have had an argument with your spouse, and before it was over, you couldn't even remember how the argument even got started?

The enemy wants to keep husbands and wives divided and upset with each other (not in unity, where God would have us). The enemy knows the power there is in unity between a husband and wife, and he knows what strife will do.

It is time that, we, as believers, realize that the same strength and power in unity needs to be in our marriages. It is time that we do what we can to remain in unity with our spouses.

I am not talking about being a doormat and allowing our spouse to walk on us in order to have peace and unity. I am talking about each one of us doing our part to remain in unity. I am talking about not provoking one another into an argument or trying to irritate each other.

Unity in marriage is crucial. Where there is unity, there is strength and peace; I can't stress this enough. God keeps having me say this to you.

God has ordained unity. We are to remain in unity. When we are in unity, we are in agreement. There is power in agreement.

> Matthew 18:19-20 (NIV) reads, *"Again I tell you that if two of you on earth agree about anything you ask for, it will be done for you by My Father in heaven. For where two or three come together in My name, there I am with them."*

When we are in agreement, we are causing what is to be done, to be done. Agreement causes God to move.

Generally speaking, my husband and I are usually in agreement. If we are not in agreement on a decision that needs to be made, we do not do anything until we are. When a couple is in agreement and in unity, there is peace, power, and strength. When there is strife between a husband and a wife, then there is exactly the opposite: less peace, less power, and less strength. Leviticus 26:8 (NIV) says, *"Five of you will chase a hundred, and a hundred of you will chase ten thousand, and your enemies will fall by the sword before you.*

This is what happens when there is agreement: multiplied power and strength.

Unity is crucial in a marriage; husbands and wives need to be in agreement and be a unified force.

Colossians 3:14 (NIV) says, *"Above all, clothe yourselves with love, which binds us all together in perfect harmony."*

Walk in *love* with your spouse. Love will bind you together in perfect harmony. Harmony is agreement and oneness.

> Ephesians 4:3 reads, *"Make every effort to keep the unity of the Spirit through the bond of peace."*

It is important to remember to walk in unity with your spouse. Think about this: God the Father, God the Son, and God the Holy Spirit are all in unity. We are to follow Christ's example.

> I Peter 2:21 *states, "To this you were called because Christ suffered for you, leaving you an example, that you should follow in His steps."*

Ecclesiastes 4:12 says, *"Though one may be overpowered, two can defend themselves. A cord of three strands is not quickly broken."* This is why unity is important – a triple-braided cord is stronger than a double-braided cord, and it will not be easily broken.

You, your spouse, and the Holy Spirit all unified together will not easily be broken. We need to remain in unity with one another, and partner with God and the Holy Spirit. We will be a force to be reckoned with.

The devil knows the strength that a married couple has when they are in unity, that's why he goes after marriages. Let's be as wise as a serpent to his schemes, not give in to them, and remain in unity with our spouses. Knowing this motivates me even more to remain in unity with my spouse and everyone else. I will not and cannot let the devil think he has won or gained any ground in my life or my marriage. Jesus defeated him at the cross, and he remains defeated. He has absolutely no power unless we give it to him. Jesus stripped him of *all* power.

So, with that said, let's agree to remain in unity with our spouses and others.

> Psalm 34:14 *says, "Turn from evil and do good; seek peace and pursue it."* Let's all seek peace and pursue it together.

> Lord, help us to remain in unity with our spouses and everyone else. Help us to be strong and not give in to the devil's schemes. Help us, Lord, to be a unified force for You.

> In Jesus's name,
Amen.

Chapter 3

WHY IS UNITY SO IMPORTANT IN MARRIAGE?

We have covered this topic some in the previous chapter, but now, let's look at it more extensively. There have been times in my own marriage when my husband and I were not in agreement with one another; and actually, we were at odds with each other, and that gave the enemy access. When we, as married couples, are in strife with one another or arguing, it can open the door for the enemy. It isn't God who is opening the door for the enemy or allowing him in, it is us (when we are in strife or arguing). This is why the enemy tries to cause husbands and wives to be in strife and argue with one another. He knows what it does. He also knows that when husbands and wives remain in unity with one another, we have a stronger bond, and our prayers and decisions are stronger.

Psalm 34:14 reads, *"Turn from evil and do good; seek peace and pursue it."*

> Proverbs 15:1 *says, "A gentle answer turns away wrath, but a harsh word stirs up anger."*

These are instructions from the Lord on what to do and how to handle strife when it tries to come between us.

We are to seek peace and pursue it. We are to answer anger with a gentle answer. A gentle answer will turn wrath away. How can someone continue to argue with a person who will not argue back? So, whether you feel as though you are right or wrong, choose to seek peace and pursue it at all times. Turn from evil and do good. Turn from arguing with your spouse, and turn from strife. Do not give the devil any access into your life or marriage. Cut off strife quickly, and put a stop to it.

As I was sitting and thinking about unity, and the unity between a husband and wife, the Lord brought this to mind: How many of you remember the game "Red Rover?" In that game, we locked hands with the one on either side of us and stood our ground waiting for a player from the opposing side to run and break through. If you had a solid grip on your teammates' hands, and vice versa, the opposing player could not break through that hold. They could not break through the unified force they were coming against.

Unity in marriage is kind of like this analogy. If you are unified with your spouse, you create that unified force, and the enemy, when he comes against either of you, cannot break through.

When we are in agreement with our spouses, it is like locking hands with each other and standing together against our common opponent; he cannot break through if he tries.

When there is unity (agreement), there is peace; however, where there is strife, the Bible says there is *every* form of evil (James 3:16).

I can only speak for myself, but I would rather have peace. I would rather lock hands with my husband and be that unified force.

> James 3:16 (NIV) says, *"For where you have envy and selfish ambition, there you find disorder and every evil practice."*
>
> James 3:16 in the KJV reads, *"For where envying and strife is, there is confusion and every evil work."*
>
> And, Psalm 133:1 states, *"How good and pleasant it is when brothers live together in unity."*

Do you see the contrast of living in envy and strife, versus unity? I choose unity and not strife.

Understand this: this does not mean you are to be a doormat for your spouse to walk on. No, this means you are trying to live in peace by living in unity. Pray together, seek God together, and consider each other's feelings at all times. Don't seek to have your own way, and to always be right. Instead, have the attitude of, "What can I do to stay in peace and in unity with my spouse? What can I do to bless my spouse today? What can I do to enhance our marriage and our lives together?"

Put your spouse *above* yourself. Put your spouse's needs above your own. If you both do this, you are not seeking things for yourselves, but for each other. You will have unity and peace in your marriage, your lives, and your household! Make it a goal in your marriage to live in unity – you will not be disappointed with the results.

I am a firm believer in the fact that unity is vitally important in a marriage. Agreement is crucial. Where there is unity, there is peace, I cannot stress this enough. This is one reason that the enemy, the devil, tries to keep married couples at odds with each other. If unity in marriage was not vital and important, why would the devil be fighting marriage so hard? Look at the divorce rate in America. In 2014, the divorce rate was fifty percent. That is an extremely high number.

There is tremendous power in agreement between a husband and wife. That is why the enemy fights us so bad. He wants to destroy our marriages and families. He knows how vitally powerful and important a strife-free marriage is.

Jesus Christ is our example for this. See I Peter 2:21, which says, *"To this you were called, because Christ suffered for you, leaving you an example that you should follow in His steps."*

Jesus endured hardships such as persecution and ridicule. We should love one another and express that love, just like Jesus did, no matter how we are treated. When we express love – true, unconditional love – as Christ did, we are following His example. After all, in Romans 2:4, it says, "It's the goodness of God, that leads to repentance."

> Romans 2:4 states, *"Or do you show contempt for the riches of His kindness, tolerance, and patience, not realizing that God's kindness leads you toward repentance?"*

One of our goals should be to remain in unity with our spouse. One way to accomplish this is to remember I Peter 2:21, and follow Christ's example.

The enemy, the devil, knows there is strength in a unified marriage. Remember John 10:10, which states, *"The thief comes to steal, kill, and destroy – but Jesus came to give us life, and life to the full."* The devil tries to put conflict between a husband and wife because he came to steal our peace, our joy, and the unity we have. But, Glory to God, Jesus wants to give us life and life to the full.

Let's take on the perspective of Jesus, and follow His example in all things. When we get in situations and circumstances with our spouse that may lead to trouble, let's stop and ask Jesus how He would handle the situation. Let's stop and seek God before we speak or react.

Husbands and wives must work to remain unified. Make it your goal to treat your spouse with love, honor, and respect in all situations and circumstances. Remain focused on Jesus and remember He is our example to follow.

I've been in conflict with my husband before and I hate it. Conflict is the work of the enemy. If you begin to see it rising up between you, put a stop to it quickly. Do not allow the enemy to steal your joy and peace. Remain unified as a couple.

I've personally been on both sides of this coin. I have been in total unity with my husband, Jay, but I've also been in a place with Jay that had absolutely no unity. Having no unity, with strife and unrest present, is terrible. When I've gotten into a place like this with Jay, it only led to even worse things, such as emotional hurt, anger, resentment, and etc. I hope you can see the importance of remaining at peace and in unity.

On the other side of this coin, when Jay and I are in unity with each other, there is peace, joy, love, strength, power, etc. There are significant differences with being in opposition and being in complete unity and harmony.

When there is peace, joy, and unity between a husband and wife, there is power. It is an amazing place to be. Nehemiah 8:10b says, *"Do not grieve, for the joy of the Lord is your strength."*

> Psalm 34:14 states, *"Turn from evil and do good; seek peace and pursue it."*

According to the Word of God, we are to seek peace and pursue it. Run from strife, and pursue peace. Run after God! This, ladies and gentlemen, should be the goal we go after, and the lifestyle we live. You will be amazed at the difference in your marriage and also your personal life. They will not be the same.

Romans 14:19 says, *"Let us therefore make every effort to do what leads to peace and to mutual edification,"* (Greek; "building up, strengthening").

Make every effort to remain in peace in your personal life and with your spouse. Make it your goal to edify your spouse, to strengthen them, and build them up, instead of tearing them down. We all need an "Atta boy" or "Atta girl" once in a while.

We all need affirmation. Be your spouse's encourager. Encourage them to be all God has called them to be.

Seek peace and pursue it. Run after God; He is waiting for you.

Let's pray!

> Father, I ask You now to help me to remain at peace with (spouse's name). Help me to see (spouse's name) the way You see him/her. Give me the words to encourage him/her to be all You have called them to be.
>
> In the name of Jesus,
> Amen.

Chapter 4

GOD'S PLAN FOR MARRIAGE

Genesis 2:20-24 states:

So the man gave names to all the livestock, the birds of the air and the beasts of the field. But for Adam no suitable <u>helper</u> was found. So the Lord God caused the man to fall into a deep sleep, and while he was sleeping, He took one of the man's ribs and closed up the place with flesh. Then the Lord God made a woman from the rib He had taken out of the man, and He brought her to the man. The man said, "This is now bone of my bone and flesh of my flesh; she shall be called woman, for she was taken out of man." For this reason a man will leave his father and mother and be <u>united</u> to his wife, and they will become <u>one flesh</u> (underlining added by me).

God's design for marriage is for the husband and wife to become *one* flesh. We are to be one with our spouse.

We are to become one body – we complete each other, with Christ in the center, of course.

Mark 10:8-9 says, *"And the two will become one flesh. Therefore what God has joined together, let man not separate."*

<u>Joined together</u> in the Greek dictionary means, "with; as; beside; to connect."

When we marry, we are to remain beside our spouse. We are to be as they are; we are connected with them. Marriage was designed by God and is a powerful covenant. Marriage was designed by God to provide partnership, spiritual intimacy, and the ability to pursue God together. Marriage mirrors God's covenant relationship with His people. Jesus refers to Himself as the "Bridegroom," (Matt. 9:15) and to the kingdom of Heaven as a "Wedding banquet," (Matt. 22:2).

God designed marriage for a purpose. Ladies and gentlemen, marriage is a *God*-thing. It is a covenant, and one not to be taken lightly.

Marriage is a partnership. It is a covenant; it isn't a contract or agreement. Marriage is meant to be a lifetime covenant, not a contract that can be cancelled by an attorney.

Marriage was designed by God as a covenant, a lifelong commitment between husband and wife. Husbands and wives are meant to complement one another, build each other up, and to draw out of each other what God has put in them.

Marriage is a union from God that is meant to last for the rest of our lives; it is not a contract that can be broken or cancelled at any time. Marriage is a union that is a powerful force when husbands and wives are in unity. There is great power in the unity between a husband and wife; however, it must be in submission to God's plan for you.

Ephesians 5:22 states:

> *Wives, submit to your husbands as to the Lord. For the husband is the head of the wife as Christ is the head of the church, His body of which He is the Savior. Now as the church submits to Christ, so also wives should submit to their husbands in everything.*

And, *Ephesians 5:25-28 reads:*

> *Husbands, love your wives just as Christ loved the church and gave Himself up for her to make her holy, cleansing her by the washing with water through the Word, and to present her to Himself as a radiant church, without stain or wrinkle or any blemish, but holy and blameless. In this same way, husbands ought to love their wives as their own bodies. He who loves his wife loves himself.*

This is how marriage should be: wives should submit to their husbands as to the Lord in everything, and husbands should love their wives as Christ loves the church (a side note: submission is *not* demeaning; it is honorable).

Ladies, God designed marriage for the husband to be the leader. He is your spiritual covering. This is not to say that wives do not have a spiritual input. Husbands, you are to love your wives as Christ loved the church.

Marriage is designed to reflect or mirror God's covenant relationship with His people, His children. As we are one with God, so we are to be one with each other (man/husband with woman/wife). We are meant to have a relationship with Jesus Christ, first and foremost, then with our spouse. We are to keep Christ in the center of our individual lives, and in the center of our marriages.

> Ecclesiastes 4:12 says, *"Though one may be overpowered, two can defend themselves. A cord of three strands is not quickly broken."*

There is a plan and *purpose* for marriage, set up by God. With a Christ-centered, Christ-focused marriage, there is fulfillment, joy, peace, unity, and satisfaction.

God designed marriage for partnership and intimacy (with God and with each other), and the ability to run after (pursue) God together. He also designed marriage to be a unified force. I say again that marriage is a covenant between one man and one woman. Unlike what the world portrays, marriage should be for life.

Let's look at the difference between a contract and a covenant:

Contract – An agreement forced by law; an agreement between two or more parties for the doing or not doing of something specified; the formal agreement of marriage. A contract creates a legal duty or responsibility.

Covenant – A binding agreement or contract between two or more parties; in legal terms, it is a formal sealed agreement or contract. (I found this: a covenant is a relationship between two parties who make binding promises to each other and work together to reach a common goal. They're often accompanied by oaths, signs, and ceremonies. Covenants define obligations and commitments, but they are different from a contract because they are relational and personal).

When we marry, we are *in covenant* with our spouse; it is not merely a contract. Marriage is meant to be for life.

The world's system has made it easy to get out of a marriage through divorce (this is not God's plan). Many couples have decided to get a divorce because it is easier to get a divorce than stay and fight for their marriage.

I encourage you, if your marriage is struggling, don't give up. Your marriage is worth fighting for. Go to God in prayer for your marriage, and make sure God is the center of your individual life, and the center of your marriage. Give God a chance to help you work things out. Please don't quit; don't throw in the towel. FIGHT! FIGHT! FIGHT! Your marriage is worth fighting for.

In my own personal life, at one point, our marriage was really bad for a while. Our flesh wanted to quit, but we couldn't give up and throw in the towel. We chose to fight for our marriage, and we dedicated our lives to God and to following His will for us.

I am so thankful today that we didn't quit. I am here to tell you today, that I have an amazing marriage. Our marriage is flourishing. It is better than it has ever been, and it just keeps getting better and better.

We would have missed an amazing life together if we had quit. Today, we are traveling together, preaching the gospel, laying hands on the sick, and seeing God heal and work miracles. This was His divine plan for my husband, myself, and our marriage. This was God's plan for us; had we quit and divorced we would have thwarted and stopped His plan.

> Isaiah 55:9 says, *"As the Heavens are higher than the earth, so are My ways higher than your ways and My thoughts than your thoughts."*
>
> Proverbs 16:9 reads, *"In his heart a man plans his course, but the Lord determines His steps."*

If your marriage is in a bad spot, will you please consider these scriptures? Stop, pray, and allow the Lord to speak to you. Allow Him to work in your marriage. There is nothing too big for God. Matthew 19:26 says, *"Jesus looked at them and said, 'With man this is impossible, but with God all things are possible.'"*

God has healed and restored my marriage, and it is better by far than it ever was. Don't give up – Jesus is the center of my life, my husband's life, and my marriage. Put God first and foremost in your life and in your marriage, and see what He will do. Allow Him to be the center of your life and marriage. As you do this, you will never be the same. I can say this because this is exactly what has happened to me, my husband, and our marriage.

There is so much power between a husband and wife that are in unity with each other and with God. Why do you think the devil wants to destroy marriages?

I would like to share a personal example of this, of how the enemy tried to destroy a marriage and why. My husband, Jay, and I got married at the ages of sixteen and seventeen. We were going along great for a while, then it changed. The enemy attacked our marriage, and tried to destroy and divide it. I will honestly say, it was bad. But, Jay and I wouldn't quit. There were times our flesh wanted to quit; it was a battle. It was a battle for *years*. The enemy attacked us and our marriage severely.

After many years, we began to see some victory and progress in our lives and marriage. First, let me say that our marriage was in this condition because Jay and I were not where we could have been spiritually. Yes, we would go to church some, but didn't make a firm commitment.

When we did make that commitment, the battle didn't stop. Why? Because we had opened the door for the enemy to attack by choices we had made in our lives *prior* to changing our commitment to Christ. After we first began seeking His kingdom (Matt. 6:33), the battle continued. We were both saved, but we weren't totally sold out for Jesus; we weren't running after Him. Once we began turning our lives toward Jesus and running after Him, things began to change.

My mother-in-law, Martha, was a great help through this battle. She is an amazing woman of God, one who shows the love of Jesus constantly. She was always there for both of us. I love you!

We tried Christian counseling, which helped a little. The thing that helped the most was committing our lives to Jesus.

We found an amazing church to attend, and began the process of restoration. Our pastors, Leo and Linda Morgan, were greatly used by God to restore our marriage. Pastors Leo and Linda, we are eternally grateful for the two of you, for investing your time into our lives and marriage. You were greatly used by God to restore our marriage. We love you both so much.

Now, our marriage is tremendous. Jay and I travel all over, sharing the Gospel of Jesus Christ, praying for the sick, seeing God heal them and setting the captives free, all for God's glory!

Had we given up and not fought for our marriage, we would have missed out on so much. What the Lord had intended for our marriage and for us would not have manifested.

My point is this: God had great plans for Jay and myself. The enemy tried to destroy those plans and prevent them from happening before Jay and I even knew about them. But, God knew!

Hosea 4:6 says, *"My people are destroyed from lack of knowledge."* We were almost destroyed, because we were not putting ourselves in a position to know what the enemy was doing and to know the Word of God, and our marriage was almost destroyed.

God, with His great love, mercy, and grace, saved our marriage. Not only did He save our marriage, but He restored our marriage. Our marriage today is better than it has ever been, and it keeps getting better.

> Genesis 50:20 (NLT) says, *"You intended to harm me, but God intended it all for good. He brought me to this position so I could save the lives of many people."*

God had a plan and purpose for Jay, myself, and our marriage. From the beginning, the enemy tried to destroy it, but God brought us to the place we are today. God had a plan and purpose and the enemy was not able to thwart that plan because we gave our lives to God and surrendered to His will.

James 4:7 says, *"Submit yourselves then to God, resist the devil and he will flee from you."* The first thing Jay and I had to do was *submit to God*. Then, we could resist the devil, and he would flee from us.

God restored what the enemy had tried to do to our marriage. He not only restored it, He has made it better, and continues to make it better and better. We walk in unity with each other and with God.

God has a plan for your marriage and for the both of you. Don't throw it away. Fight the good fight of faith; submit to God, resist the devil, and he will flee.

You are more than a conqueror in Christ Jesus. Greater is He that is in you than he that is in the world. You can do it!

Chapter 5

THE ROLE OF THE HUSBAND

*H*usbands and wives have God-given roles in the marriage that they are meant to fill. In this chapter, I will address the husband's role, then, in the next chapter, I will address the wife's role.

When we step up and fulfill our God-given roles, it helps bring peace and unity into our marriage. Men have a desire to lead their wives, and they also have a desire and need for respect from their wives. Wives have a desire to be led by their husbands, and a desire and need for love and affection from their husbands.

When we fulfill these needs and desires for our spouse, it brings peace and unity. We, as people, have these desires and needs because that is how God created us. We each have roles and positions in our marriage to fulfill; these are God-given roles.

The husband is meant to be the spiritual leader of his household. He is meant to lead, not dominate. There is a huge difference in the two.

Colossians 3:18-19 says, *"Wives submit to your husbands, as is fitting to the Lord. Husbands, love your wives and do not be harsh with them."*

Just a note here: in the Lord, we are all equal, but God set up an order in the home and in marriage. Husbands are to be the spiritual leaders of their homes. A spiritual leader imitates Christ. Christ gave His life up for us. The husband, as the spiritual leader, means he must have a strong connection with His Heavenly Father, a close relationship with God. The husband can only lead effectively when he maintains an intimate relationship with the Lord. He needs to be balanced in his commitments and nurturing in his concerns for the mental and emotional needs of each family member. He must be proactive in the welfare of his wife and children, and helpful with solutions to potential problems. He must also be characterized by integrity.

Now, ladies, I want to interject a side note here for you. Your husband can lead you well, but it will be helpful to him if you honor and respect his role as the spiritual leader of your home and marriage, and submit to His leadership.

Ephesians 5:22-29 states:

> *Husbands, love your wives just as Christ loved the church and gave Himself up for her to make her holy, cleansing her by the washing with water through the Word, and to present her to Himself as a radiant church, without stain or wrinkle or any other blemish, but holy and*

> *blameless. In this same way, husbands ought to love their wives as their own bodies. He who loves his wife loves himself. After all, no one ever hated his own body, but he feeds and cares for it, just as Christ does the church.*

Husbands, you are the head of your wife and your home. You are the spiritual head of your household, as Christ is the head of the church. You are meant to love your wives, as Christ loved the Church and gave Himself up for it. The Word of God says you are to love your wife as your own body. The Word also says above, "He who loves his wife, loves himself." After all, no one ever hated his own body, but he feeds and cares for it, just as Christ does the Church – for we are members of His body.

> Ephesians 5:31 says, *"For this reason a man will leave his father and mother and be united with his wife, and the two will become one flesh."*

God has given you a tremendous but wonderful position as the spiritual head of your wife and home. God is entrusting you to lead your wife and household in the ways of God, to cover them in prayer, to love them as Christ loved the Church, and to treasure them as well.

Wives desire love and affection from their husbands. They want affirmation from their husbands. Men, compliment your wives, tell them you love them; and remember, a hug or a gentle touch from you carries a lot of weight. Women want to know their husbands love them and treasure them as friends and wives. They want to know you appreciate them.

Yes, your wife is to submit to you and honor and respect you.

Remember this: it is easier for a wife to honor you, respect you, and be a good wife, if she has a good leader. Don't misunderstand me; we, as wives, are to honor, respect, and submit to our husbands, whether we feel like they deserve it or not. My husband has said that, "If you want your wife to be a submitted wife, be easy to submit to; be a good leader."

Men, you have an important position in your home and marriage; you are to lead your home in a godly manner. You are the provider, protector, and supporter. You are your family's spiritual covering. Your family needs you to lead them in the Lord.

> 1 Peter 3:7 reads, *"Husbands, in the same way be considerate with your wives, and treat them with respect as the weaker partner and as heirs with you of the gracious gift of life, so that nothing will hinder your prayers."*

This scripture is not saying your wife is worthless. It is simply saying that she was not created to do some of the things you were created to do. She was not created to lead your home – you were. She wasn't created to be the spiritual leader of your home – you were.

Men, you were created to lead your wife and family in the Lord. You are to honor and cherish them. As you do this, you will see your wife follow you, submit to you, and honor and respect you.

You are your wife's spiritual covering. You are meant to lead her in Christ. You are designed to be the spiritual head of your house. She looks to you to lead her, love her, cherish her, and support her. I know: big job, right? It is much easier to lead your wife, love, cherish, and support her, if you are led by the Lord, and by His Holy Spirit.

Men, it is so important for you, as well as everyone, to spend your quiet private time with the Lord.

Your wife will absolutely love it when you lead her in the Lord. I do! I love that my husband leads me spiritually; I love that he is my covering.

What makes a good follower? A good leader. Both require submission to God.

Women want someone to lead them, love them, and cherish them. They want someone to take charge, to lead, but not dominate and control. Wives need leadership in the ways of the Lord.

> Ephesians 5:23 says, *"For the husband is the head of the wife as Christ is the head of the church, His body, of which He is the Savior."*

You are to be the head (leader) of your wife, just as Christ is for the Church. Christ gave Himself up for us. Christ loves and cares for us, and the church (Ephesians 5:29).

Men, please take time to read and study Ephesians 5:22-23; it will help to open your understanding of your role. You have a God-given role in your household, and with your wife. Spend time with God so He can show you how to lead them. Christ is your example. Learn who He is and *how* He is. Learn who you are in Him. He leads with love, because He is love.

I love my husband to lead me. I love that he runs after Jesus, and because he runs after Jesus, I know that he will lead me and my family, as God desires us to be led.

As you lead your wife in the Lord, she will follow. Wives were not created to lead their husbands; husbands were created to lead their wives. Praise God that I was not created to be the head (spiritual leader) of my house.

Being the head of your home and your wife means being the spiritual leader. It is a very important role and position in the household. Wives need this leadership from you. Lead your wife as Christ leads the Church; be a godly example. Love her, cherish her, care for her, pray for and *with* her, and seek Christ with and *for* her. She will honor and respect you for it.

Men, as you embark on this journey, or even if you are already on this journey, my prayer for you is this:

> "Father, I pray that You give the husbands and men who are seeking You in the area of leading their wives, the spirit of wisdom and revelation in this area. Speak to them, Holy Spirit, on how to lead, love, direct, and cherish their wives. Empower them, God, to lead their wives and households in You. Show them what this looks

like. Father, show them how to lead their wives and households the way that You want them led."

In Jesus's Name,
Amen!

Men, lean on Jesus to help you. Ask Holy Spirit to reveal to you the plan He has for you, your marriage and your household. He will show you the way.

> In John 14:6, Jesus said, *"I am the way and the truth and the life. No one comes to the Father except through Me."*

Husbands and men, this is what the Lord spoke to me for you to be put at the end of this chapter. The Lord gave me this scripture and said to me, "This Word (scripture) is for the men and husbands who desire to lead their wives and households in Me. I will direct their steps and ways as they seek Me and desire to walk in My ways."

> Isaiah 30:21 reads, *"Whether you turn to the right or to the left, your ears will hear a voice behind you saying, 'This is the way; walk in it.'"*

Men, this is for *you*, directly from God: Trust Him to lead you. Trust Him to guide you, and show you the way to lead and guide your wives and families.

Chapter 6

THE ROLE OF THE WIFE

Well, wives, let's get right to it: We are to honor, respect, and submit to our husbands.

Ephesians 5:22-24 states:

> *Wives, submit to your husbands as to the Lord. For the husband is the head of the wife as Christ is the head of the church, His body of which He is Savior. Now as the church submits to Christ, so also wives should submit to their husbands in everything.*

Let's look at a few things in these scriptures:

1) We are to submit to our husbands, as to the Lord.
2) The husband is head of the wife, as Christ is head of the Church.
3) We are to submit to our husbands, as the Church submits to Christ.

4) We are to submit to our husbands in everything. (Note: we are not required by God to submit to our husbands in things that do not line up with the Word, or are ungodly).

Let me also take this time to interject this scripture:

"Your attitude should be the same as that of Christ Jesus." – Philippians 2:5

Ladies, Christ Jesus submitted to His Father, even unto death. He had an attitude of submission and love – *unconditional* love. Many women today think that if they submit to their husbands, that it is demeaning, and it makes them feel as though they do not have a say or a place of importance. That is the furthest thing from the truth. When we submit to our husbands, we are being obedient to God and are honoring our husbands; we are being as Christ is, and are humbling ourselves.

Submission is beautiful, honorable, humbling, and obedient to God. Submission allows our husbands to take the position God has given them and called them to do.

Submission to our husbands not only honors them, but honors God. Think about Jesus Christ and His submission to God – even unto death. Look what His submission did for us. It brought us forgiveness of sins, healing, redemption, grace, deliverance, sanctification, and the list goes on.

Submission is not something we, as women, should dread or hate doing, because ultimately, submission to our husbands goes beyond merely submitting to our husbands; it is also submitting to God. How can I say these things? I can say this because God instructed us to submit to our husbands, as unto the Lord. I am not saying it is always easy, but it is always possible. As we submit to God first, it will be easier to submit to our husbands.

Scripture doesn't say to submit to our husbands only when we think they deserve it or when we feel like it. No, we are to live a life of submission to our husbands. However, we do not and *are not* required to submit if our husbands are asking us to do something that is ungodly, or does not line up with the Word of God.

Colossians 3:18 says, *"Wives, submit to your husbands, as is fitting in the Lord."* This is instruction from the Lord. Submission was designed by God to lead us into a beautiful relationship with our husbands. Jesus is the ultimate example of submission – even unto death. Submission without complaint results in tremendous blessings. God told us to submit to our husbands, to honor them, and respect them. I promise that if you will do this, you will reap tremendous results. It is one thing to be obedient, but it is another to be *willing* and obedient. Isaiah 1:19 says, *"If you are willing and obedient, you will eat the good things of the land."*

It isn't only about obedience; it's also willingness. I can do things out of obedience to God, and do it begrudgingly. If that is my attitude, then I shouldn't even do it. But, if I do it willingly and obediently, then that is different, and will bring different results.

It isn't always easy to submit, but it is necessary; scripture tells us to submit, so we should submit with love, respect, and honor. Husbands like it when we submit to them, not so they can lord it over us or dominate us, but because God designed them to need this. Women were designed by God to need and want love, affection, and to be cherished. This is God's designed plan and His way.

We, as women and wives, need to focus on our God-given role, and fulfilling that role, which is honoring, respecting, loving, and complementing our husbands, and being their helpmeet. Many women desire love, affection, and support from their husbands, but do not show them the love, honor, and respect they need. This is not what God intended.

Your role, wives, is to be your husbands' companion, friend, helper, lover, greatest supporter, and cheerleader. Your husband needs to know that he is first (*after* God, of course) in your life, the most important person in your life.

Here is a revelation that my husband, Jay, received: you are not complete without your husband, and he is not complete without you. You complete each other. When you married, you became one!

> Mark 10:7-8 says, *"For this reason a man will leave his father and mother and be united to his wife and the two will become one flesh. So they are no longer two, but one flesh."*

You complete each other. You become one. What you do or do not do affects your husband and vice-versa.

There is a reason God designed a husband and wife to become *one* – for the purpose of completing each other.

My husband and I are best friends. We can work, play, preach, and hang out together twenty-four-seven, and it is wonderful. We are companions, spouses, and friends. It is a great thing to be your husband's best friend, ladies.

When your husband has a moment of weakness or struggles, you are meant to come along and be his strength, to hold him up in prayer, and support him. Ultimately, his strength comes from the Lord and so does yours, but you are meant to help each other.

There have been times in our marriage when I was weak and I needed my husband to be strong for us both. This is what I am talking about. Be your husband's best friend, and be someone he can confide in, someone he can trust, someone he can lean on, pray with, or just come and hang out with. Life is a blast, ladies, when you fulfill the roles that God has given you as a husband and wife.

I love being my husband Jay's wife. I love being his friend and his companion. I love being there for him when he needs me. Our life together is amazing. We have an incredible marriage and relationship. It hasn't always been that way, but the fact is: now it is absolutely incredible. We have learned through the years how to be the wife and husband God designed us to be.

I'm encouraging you ladies to study your husband. Learn who he is, what he likes, what he doesn't like, what you can do to minister to him, and how you can help him be all God intended him to be. Pray and ask God what you can do to help complete your husband. Ask God to help you be the wife He has called you to be, and the wife your husband needs and desires.

As you begin to do the things we have talked about, you will be amazed at the change it produces in you, your husband, and your marriage. It works; I have done it!

Ladies, let's be real. How many of us want our husbands to love us unconditionally, show us affection regularly, cherish us, want to spend time with us, and put us first? I believe I can answer this for us all – we all do. So, let's begin to sow into our husbands what we desire to receive from them. Let's begin to honor them, respect them, cherish them, love them unconditionally, spend time with them, and regularly show them affection. You will be surprised at what you receive in return.

Now, let me clarify this: you can't expect to do this one time and see a major difference right away. In Galatians 6:7-9, the Word of God says we will reap what we sow:

> *Don't be misled-you cannot mock the justice of God. You will always harvest what you plant. Those who live only to satisfy their own sinful nature will harvest decay and death from that sinful nature. But those who live to please the Spirit will harvest everlasting life from the Spirit. So let's not get tired of doing what is good. At just the right time we will reap a harvest of blessing if we don't give up.*

This doesn't only apply to money. This applies to everything.

Let's take a moment to think about a garden or a crop; you first plant the seed, then the seed must be watered. As you water the seed, the vegetable or fruit begins to grow. It takes time, but you will reap a harvest.

As you begin to do these things with and *for* your husband, and continue to do them, you will receive what you seek in return. Begin to pray and focus on what you can do to improve your relationship with your husband. Begin to pray and focus on what you can do to minister to your husband. Then, do what God shows you. Stop focusing on what you aren't getting and what he isn't doing. Focus instead on what you can give, not what you can get.

Marriage isn't about give and take. It isn't 50/50. It is about give, and give some more. It is 100/100. If you both focus on *giving* to one another instead of taking or on what you can get, things will change. If you both focus on giving 100% all the time, then you will see the results.

You will complete each other. You will fulfill your God-given role in your marriage. Your relationship with your spouse will flourish; it will be what you desire, and what God has planned for you. Begin to focus on your role as a wife, instead of focusing on your husband fulfilling his role. Begin to seek the Lord on what you can do as the wife to minister to your husband. Shift your focus to fulfilling your role in the marriage. Ask the Lord to help you become all you are destined to be, both as a wife and as a woman of God. If you haven't already done so, put your relationship with God first.

The Role of the Wife

Your role as a wife is so important. God has placed the honor of being a wife into your life. He will help you become the best wife you can be.

I can testify that being a wife, a godly wife, is an incredible, fulfilling life. But, it doesn't stop there. You are called by God. He has a destiny for you to walk in. Draw close to Him and be the best *you* that you can be. Allow who God has called you to be to come forth.

Father God,

I pray for all the wives and women who are reading this. I pray that You help them and give them revelation on how to be the woman and wife You are calling them to be. I declare that these women will walk in their role to the fullest. I declare that they will be all You have called them to be. Father, I ask You to give them a supernatural strength to become the mighty women that You are calling them to be. Father, help them to see who they are in You. Father, teach each one of them how to be the best wife they can be, and how to let out the mighty woman of God that is inside them.

In the mighty name of Jesus, I pray,
Amen!

Chapter 7

THE ROLE OF GOD IN MARRIAGE

In this chapter, I am going to share a personal experience in my own marriage. I want to explain to you, by my own experience, the importance of having God in the center of our marriages. First, He must be at the center of our individual lives, and then our marriages.

My husband, Jay, and I have been married since we were sixteen and seventeen. At the writing of this book, we have been married for forty years. I would love to tell you that those forty years were perfect, but I can't.

At one point in our marriage, it was terrible. But, with that said, as bad as it was, we refused to divorce; it was not an option. We both were responsible for it being so terrible. One thing was definite in those years: we <u>did</u> <u>not</u> have God first in our lives or our marriage.

When we made the choice to put God first in our individual lives and in our marriage, things began to turn around. It was not an overnight fix; it took time. But, today, my husband and I have a tremendous marriage and relationship. We each began to run after God and put Him first in our own lives, and then we placed Him in the center of our marriage. For years now, Jay and I have been best friends, and our relationship is solid and secure on *our rock*, Jesus Christ. We have never been happier, and our relationship with each other has never been this secure and stable, or as great.

God belongs first in our individual lives, and then in our marriages. He needs to be the center of it all. God's desire is to be close to us, to be our Father, our Daddy. It is up to us to invite and allow Him to be near us.

James 4:8 says, *"Come near to God and He will come near to you."* God is waiting for you! He is waiting for you to draw near to Him. God is a gentleman; He will not force His way in. But, if you draw near to Him and allow Him to come in and help you, He will.

When my husband and I began to draw near to God, put Him first, and allow Him to help and work in our lives, things began to change and turn around. Today, we have a wonderful marriage and relationship.

We cannot change our spouses, but God can. When we step out of the way and allow God to work, He changes us and our spouse. If we try to change our spouse instead of allowing God to change them, we will only be frustrated and disappointed, but if we allow God to change them, we will see the results. God is waiting for you to take your hands off of the situations in your life, and off of your spouse, so He can do what He is waiting to do and wants to do on your behalf. He is a good, good Father who only wants the best for you and your spouse. God wants to see your marriage flourish more than you do.

God desires to bless you and your marriage with all of His goodness. He wants you to have peace and joy. He's waiting for you and me to let Him in, and for us to move out of the way so he can do what He desires to do.

God's design is for your marriage to flourish and thrive. Marriage is ordained by God. If He ordained it, He will bless it. So many times, we are ones the who get in the way by trying to *fix* our spouse. Fixing our spouse, as we might call it, is God's job, not ours. And when we are the ones trying to *fix* them instead of allowing God to do what *He* wants to do in our spouses, we only cause problems and strife, and block God from doing what *He* wants to do, and what *He* knows is best. We are not our spouses' Holy Spirit.

It is time that we move out of the way and allow God to do what He wants to do in our lives, our spouses' lives, and our marriages. It is time that we give God His rightful place.

Allow God to do what He wants to do in your spouse, in you, and in your marriage. He has so much in store for you. But, when we try to step in and take God's place in our spouses' lives, we interfere and are actually blocking God from doing what He wants to do. We get in the way.

God desires and wants to be first place in your life, your spouse's life, and in your marriage. When we allow Him to have that place, then He can do what He desires and wants to do.

Ladies and gentlemen, you cannot change each other – but God can! Step back, repent (ask God to forgive you for trying to be Him to your spouse), move out of God's way, and let Him work and move. You will be amazed at what happens. God will move and your marriage will become even better than you could imagine. My marriage is proof.

> John 10:10 (NKJV) says, *"The thief does not come except to steal, and to kill, and to destroy. I have come that they may have life, and that they may have it more abundantly."*

The devil – who is the thief – comes to steal, kill, and destroy, not God. God comes to give you life, and life more abundantly. So, if you, your spouse, and your marriage are not experiencing life, and life more abundantly, then you know who is at work.

Allow God to have first place in your life and your marriage. How do you do this?

1) By seeking Him first above anyone or anything.
2) By stepping out of His way.
3) By placing God as the most important person in your life.
4) By allowing God to change you and your spouse instead of you trying to do it.

These are only a few things we can do.

God is truly not about rules and regulations, the do's and do not's. He is about *relationship*. As we draw close to God and put Him first in our lives and our marriages, we show Him we are trying to do the right thing out of love for Him.

God should be first and foremost in our individual life, and the most important person in our marriage. As a husband and wife are both running after God independently, it draws them closer to each other. As your individual relationships with God get stronger, your marriages will get stronger. As your marriage gets stronger, unity grows.

The greatest thing you can do is to give God first place, keep Him in the center of your lives, and give Him first place in your marriage. He is the most important person in a marriage, and needs to be kept in first place in your lives *and* in your marriage. Allow Him to lead and direct you. Seek Him daily. Spend alone and quiet time with Him. Learn His voice and learn about who He is. Allow Him to help you be the best "you" possible.

God wants your lives and your marriage to be successful more than you do. He knows what you need, and He knows how to get those needs met. He is the best Teacher to show you how to treat your spouse, your children, and how to be a wife, mother, husband, and father. He is the greatest leader of all. But, we have to <u>let</u> Him lead. We have to <u>let</u> Him speak, and we have to <u>listen</u>. When He speaks and gives us instructions, we need to listen and be obedient.

God desires to speak to you, show you things, give you revelation, comfort you, lead you, direct you, and so much more. Make room for God in your daily lives, and make room for Him in your marriages. I can promise you this: if you do this, truly do this, you will not be disappointed. Keeping God in the center of your marriages is a secret to success.

We cannot change our spouses into the person we want them to be, but God can change them into who He wants them to be. By putting God first in your lives and marriages, it gives Him room to do what He wants to do in each of your lives, and in your relationship as a husband and wife.

Women, before you became wives and a mothers, you were and *are* daughters of God!

Men, before you became husbands and fathers, you were and *are* sons of God!

Do not forget your identity as daughters and sons of God. Your position at work, at your church, and in your home, is not your identity. Your identity is that you are a son or daughter of the King of kings. Enjoy your position. Receive from your Heavenly Father; He has so much for you. He is waiting for you.

Some of you only need to rest in your Daddy God's arms, and simply receive His love for you. You need to trust and believe that God has the absolute best for you and your marriage. You need to trust Him.

Don't try to change your spouse to your way. Place your spouse in the hands of God and let God do what He wants to do. We need to trust God with our spouses, get out of His way, and let Him move in our midst. He will never fail us.

He is a Daddy who can be trusted. He will never leave or forsake you (Hebrews 13:5). We need to trust God and put Him first and foremost in our lives and our marriage. You will not regret it. He will come through for you.

Proverbs 3:5-6 (NKJV) reads, *"Trust in the Lord with all your heart, and lean not on your own understanding; in all your ways acknowledge Him, and He will direct your paths."*

It is very important to keep God first every day. He will move on your behalf. God loves you and your spouse more, much more, than you love yourself or your spouse.

Success comes with God in the center. Trust me, I know. When my husband and I started putting God where He should be in our lives – which was first – everything began to change.

Don't misunderstand me; it was a process, a journey, but well worth it. My marriage is absolutely incredible. My husband and I are best friends. God transformed our lives and our marriage. Trust God, for He is trustworthy. He loves you so much. You will not regret it.

Trust Him with your spouse, and trust Him with your marriage.

Remember this: Mark 9:23 (NIV) says, *"'If you can?' said Jesus. 'Everything is possible for one who believes.'"* Matthew 19:26 (NIV) says, *"Jesus looked at them and said, 'With man this is impossible, but with God all things are possible.'"* What seems impossible to you is *possible* with God. Trust Him and keep Him in the center of your lives, and in the center of your marriages. Yield to Him, both of you, and cooperate with what He wants to do. You will not be disappointed.

Let's pray:

> Father, we ask You to forgive us when we haven't put You first in our lives or our marriages. Father, we choose today to do just that, to keep You first and foremost in our lives. Lord, today we yield to You, and we choose to cooperate with Your plan and purpose for our lives and our marriages. We tell You today that Lord, we trust You. Have Your way in our lives and in our marriages.
>
> In the mighty name of Jesus,
Amen!

Trust Him. He will never leave you or forsake you.

Chapter 8

WHERE DO WE GO FROM HERE? – UNITED FOR PURPOSE

This book is about unity in marriage, and there are so many reasons to maintain unity. There are many benefits and blessings from living and walking in unity with your spouse. You and your spouse were united for a Purpose – God's purpose.

You were put together for more than happiness, passion, and fulfillment. You were put together by God for something bigger than you: for purpose!

Purpose – The reason for which something exists or is done, made or used; an intended or desired result.

God has a desired result, and a reason He put you together.

Have you ever asked Him about His plan for you, as an individual, and as a couple? God created you to *thrive*, not merely survive. If your marriage is only surviving, I encourage you to seek God and ask Him, with an open heart and mind, what your purpose is as a woman of God, a man of God, as a spouse, and as a couple. Allow God to fulfill His divine purpose in you and in your marriage.

> Proverbs 16:9 (NIV) says, *"In their hearts humans plan their course, but the Lord establishes their steps."*
>
> And Isaiah 55:9 reads, *"For as the heavens are higher than the earth, so are My ways higher than your ways, and My thoughts than your thoughts."*

In our marriages, we get a plan and an idea of what we want our lives to be like. We plan our future many times, without even asking God about His plan for our marriages. Some even lay their entire futures out. And for many, it is exactly that, *their* plan, not God's. Many never stop and ask God what He has for them, or what His plan is for their marriage or their lives.

We go by our own plans and ways instead of God's, when, in reality, God's plans are the greatest. His plans and purposes for us are where we will be the most successful, the most satisfied, the most fulfilled, and where we will *thrive*.

A testimony from my own personal life is this: by trying to do things our way, with our plans, and not including God, not placing Him in the center – first and foremost in our marriage – our marriage was almost destroyed. However, my husband and I were too stubborn to quit. We began to do what we should have been doing all along, and that was putting God first, and in the center of our marriage, where He belonged the entire time.

When we did this, things began to shift. It didn't happen overnight, but it did happen. As we both grew with the Lord and grew closer to Him, we grew closer to each other. We began to be aligned with God and His plan for our lives, not merely our own plan. When we did this, things began to shift.

It is amazing the many ways things change when you come into alignment with God's plans and purposes for your life and marriage, instead of your own. When you and your spouse begin to lay down your plans for your lives and your marriage, and pick up God's plans for your lives, it allows Him to begin to move and take you into His plans for you. We then are taking our focus off of our plans for our marriage and lives, and putting our focus on God's plans for both. When we do this, our true destiny can begin.

One of God's goals for marriage is oneness. Genesis 2:24 (NKJV) says,

"Therefore a man shall leave his father and mother and be joined to his wife, and they shall become one flesh." One thing that will help you become one with your spouse is companionship. Spend time with your spouse; as you do, you will become more knitted together.

Praying together and discussing what you are both learning from the Lord are things that are a part of companionship and the knitting-together process. Oneness is very important in your marriage to find your purpose.

"Oneness" means: singleness; unity of thought; feeling; belief; agreement; a strong feeling of closeness of affinity; union, (definition from dictionary.com). How can we obtain oneness without companionship, without spending quality time with our spouse and allowing ourselves to be knit together?

When we were married, we became *one*. We need to do things in order to live out that oneness and purpose. If you aren't already, become your spouse's companion; pray together and share together what you are learning at church, from the Word of God, etc. Spend time together, and learn special things about each other. Oneness should be a goal for you both; after all, the scripture does say the two shall become one. Begin to strive to do these things and allow God to create that oneness. As you and your spouse pursue God and draw closer to Him, you will draw and grow closer to each other. You were united for purpose. Draw closer to Him as individuals, and as a couple, and learn what that purpose is. He has the perfect plan and divine purpose for your lives. Seek Him together to find out what that plan and purpose is. You were destined to thrive as a couple.

Your marriage has more purpose than merely spending the rest of your lives raising children together, working, having a home, etc. Your marriage is meant to mirror God's image to the world.

Genesis 1:26-27 (NIV) reads:

> *Then God said, "Let us make mankind in our own image, in our likeness, so that they may*

rule over the fish in the sea and the birds in the sky, over the livestock and all the wild animals, and over all the creatures that move along the ground." So God created mankind in His own image, in the image of God He created them, male and female, He created them.

You and your spouse are both created in the image of God. We are to reflect and resonate that image, and then, as we become one with our spouse, we are both meant to continue to run after God and pursue Him.

What God has planned and purposed for you as individuals, and as a couple, He *will* fulfill. He has a plan for you and He will do it as you pursue Him. Isaiah 14:24 (NLT) says, *"The Lord of Heaven's Armies has sworn this oath: 'It will happen as I have planned. It will be as I have decided.'"* And Isaiah 14:24 (AMPC) reads, *"The Lord of hosts has sworn, saying, 'Surely, as I have thought and planned, so shall it come to pass and as I have purposed, so shall it stand.'"* He will do it as you pursue Him and run after Him; He will do it as you submit to Him.

God has a plan and a purpose for us all. He has great things ahead for you and for your marriage.

> Jeremiah 29:11 (NLJV) says, *"'For I know the thoughts that I think toward you,' says the Lord, 'thoughts of peace and not of evil, to give you a future and a hope.'"*

I have a couple of questions for you:

1) Are you pursuing God, both as individuals, and as a couple?
2) Are you living out God's plans and purposes for your lives and your marriage?

If not, take a step, and begin to do so. Begin to look at your own life and your marriage, and see if there is any area where you are not putting God first. Look and see if there is any area, or areas, where you are trying to fulfill your own plans, purposes, and agendas before God's. If you are, begin to ask for forgiveness and allow Him to work to change things. Allow Him to fulfill His plans and purposes for you and your marriage. I can guarantee you that His plans and purposes for you and your marriage are much greater, and more fulfilling than your own.

There are reasons you are with your spouse. My husband, Jay, and I had to get our relationship with God where it should have been all along, *first*. We had to put God at the center of our marriage. When we did and we began to pursue God independently and together, things began to transform. Our marriage is so strong now. Our relationship with God and with each other is incredible. When we laid down our own agendas, our own plans and purposes, and yielded to God's agenda, plans, and purposes for our lives and marriage, everything shifted. Today, I can truly say that our marriage is incredible; it is awesome. My husband, Jay, is my best friend. Our marriage is strong. It is rooted and grounded in

God and His Word, and so are our lives. I have never in my life been more fulfilled.

I strongly encourage you to lay down your plans, agendas, purposes for your life, and for your marriage. Yield to God and allow Him to move and fulfill what He has planned and purposed for you and your marriage.

Here is a powerful truth for you: "You cannot change your spouse, but God can." My husband and I tried to change each other, and it didn't work. Now, please don't misunderstand me; you and I, and our spouses, still have to do our parts. We have things that God will require us to do. We have a role/part to play. The difference is that now we will be doing so under the leadership and guidance of God and the Holy Spirit. It is the greatest way. God's ways and thoughts are higher than ours. He will never leave us, forsake us, fail us, or disappoint us. We can trust Him with our lives and our marriages. He absolutely will change us when we yield to Him and surrender our lives, our spouses and marriages to Him. He is able to do what He wants to do with and for us.

So many things change when we yield and surrender our lives to God, when we lay down our own agendas and say, "Lord, not my agenda, but Yours; not my will, but Yours." So much can and will happen when we truly yield and give ourselves, our spouses, and our marriages to God. It allows Him to do what He wants to do and what He has planned.

Are you willing? Are you ready? Will you do these things? Do you want things to be better? Do you want to fulfill God's plans and purposes for your life and your marriage? If so, pray this prayer:

> Father, I repent for trying to do things on my own, for trying to change my spouse, and for trying to do things only You can do. I yield my life to You. I surrender my life to You. I give You myself, my spouse, and my marriage. Father, have Your way in all of these things. I lay down my plans, my way, and my agenda, and say, "Not my will, but Yours be done."
>
> In the mighty name of Jesus,
> Amen.

If you prayed this prayer and meant it, don't pick those things up again. Come into agreement with God's purpose and plan for your life, your spouse's life, and your marriage. Allow God to transform you, your spouse, and your marriage. There are no greater hands to put these things in than your Daddy God's. He will not fail you. He will not disappoint you. He will amaze you. He will overwhelm you with His love. *Trust* Him; He can be trusted. Don't look back, look ahead.

Your Daddy God has so, so much ahead for you and your marriage. Lean into Him, get to know Him, and learn who He is. Pray together with your spouse, as well as on your own. Be in the Word of God. Learn who Christ is in you and who you are in Him. Be fully committed to Him, and you will not be disappointed. He is a Father who can be *trusted*!

He can be trusted with your own life, your spouse's life, your marriage, your children, everything. He will not disappoint you. He will do above and beyond anything you ask or imagine. Just believe. Take yourself out of the way and let God be and do what He has planned and purposed for you, your spouse, your marriage, and all that pertains to you.

> Ephesians 3:20 (NKJV) says, *"Now to Him who is able to do exceedingly abundantly above all that we ask or think, according to the power that works in us."*

Let Him complete what He has prepared for you. Move on out of His way! Meaning, take your hands off of your spouse, quit trying to change them, and just let God do it. You **pray** for your spouse and for your marriage. God is able!

From my own personal marriage, my husband and I tried to change each other and *fix* things. Hear me, and hear me loud and clear: "It *didn't* work." It only brought more frustration. But, when we surrendered our own wills and truly gave our lives and our marriage to God, and got out of His way, ***wow*** is all I can say.

My marriage is incredible. It is fulfilling, satisfying, and I can truly say my husband is my best friend. It took time, but it was worth the wait. I am here to testify that it works when we truly lay everything down, stop trying to *fix* things, and believe God; He moves. He fulfills His plans and purposes for our lives and marriages when we let Him.

Release yourself, your spouse, and your marriage to God. Yield and surrender to Him. Trust Him. Believe Him. Pray! You will not be disappointed.

Chapter 9

FRIENDSHIP IN MARRIAGE

So many of us long for a friendship that is lifelong, one that will stand the test of time. One that is full of unconditional love and acceptance. I am here to say that you should and *can* have that with your spouse. Your spouse should be your best friend.

Your spouse should be second in your life, right after God, of course. God put you with your spouse for companionship, for relationship, and partnership. You were united – united for a purpose.

Let's be real here: many women and men would rather hang out with their women or men friends than their husbands or wives. This isn't how it is supposed to be. Your spouse should come before any of your friends, and before your children.

Don't misunderstand me; women and men both need friendship with other people. We all need relationships with other people. What I am saying is that your relationship with others should not come before your spouse or God. Your friends should not be the first ones you turn to. The first one you should go to is God!

Friendship in marriage between a husband and wife is an absolute. It is something that should be worked on by the husband and wife. Friendship with your spouse should be something you desire.

I love my husband dearly, and he truly is my best friend. He is the one I want to spend my time with, share my heart with, pray with, have precious moments with, and to be honest, just hang out with. We have a great friendship and relationship. It has grown stronger and stronger over the years.

We put each other second in our lives, with God first. We can work together, hang out together, be together, and enjoy each other's company twenty-four hours a day, seven days a week.

Let me say this: "God is truly your friend, your Daddy, and the One you can trust with the most intimate details of your life." There is no one I trust more than my Daddy God; He knows everything about me. I tell Him everything. He loves you and me unconditionally. You can tell Him anything and everything. He loves you unconditionally and you are fully accepted.

Friendship in marriage is so important. Mark 10:7-9 (NIV) reads, *"For this reason a man will leave his father and mother and be united to his wife, and the two will become one flesh." So, they are no longer two, but one flesh. Therefore what God has joined together, let no one separate.*

The two shall become *one* flesh. This is absolute closeness. When you married your spouse, you became united and became one flesh. That is biblical truth. Your spouse should take precedence over everyone, except God. Your relationship with your spouse takes precedence over all other relationships, except your relationship with God.

God intends and wants us to have oneness with our spouse. Oneness is possible. A key to this is keeping God in the center of your life and your marriage.

Don't misunderstand me; I am not saying women shouldn't have girlfriends and guys shouldn't have guy friends. We, as women, need our girlfriends and men need their guy friends. What I am saying is that the other relationships we have shouldn't come *before* our relationship with God or our relationship with our spouse.

If you want a stronger relationship with your spouse:

1) Be a friend to your spouse.

   Proverbs 17:17 (NKJV) says, *"A friend loves at all times, and a brother is born for adversity."*

2) Spend time together communicating on a daily basis.

   John 15:15 (NKJV) says, *"No longer do I call you servants, for a servant does not know what his master is doing; but I have called you friends, for all things that I heard from My Father I have made known to you."*

Jesus believed communication was important. He communicated all He had heard from His Father to them.

3) Reconcile conflicts.

> John 15:13 (NKJV) says, *"Greater love has no one than this, than to lay down one's life for his friends."*

> Colossians 1:21-22 (NKJV) says, *"And you, who once were alienated and enemies in your mind by wicked works, yet now He has reconciled in the body of His flesh through death, to present you holy, and blameless,* and *above reproach in His sight."*

4) Be responsive to your mate's requests.

> John 15:14 (NKJV) says, *"You show that you are my intimate friends when you obey all that I command you."*

5) Spend some recreational time together. Do fun things together.

> Song of Solomon 7:11 (NKJV) says, *"Come, my beloved, let us go forth to the field; let us lodge in the villages."*

6) Demonstrate trust.

> I Corinthians 13:7 (NIV) says, "*(Love) It always protects, always trusts, always hopes, always perseveres.*"

Many people desire their spouses to be their best friends. I can truly say from firsthand experience that it is possible. My husband and I are living it.

First, if you want your spouse to be that best friend to you, you have to be that best friend to your spouse. You need to be open in communication, responsive, and reliable. Trust is also a key in friendship. Your spouse needs to know that you can be trusted, and that they can rely on you, and you need to know these same things about your spouse.

> John 15:13 (NIV) says, "*Greater love has no one than this: to lay down one's life for one's friends.*"

> Proverbs 17:17 (NIV) says, "*A friend loves at all times, and a brother is born for a time of adversity.*"

> Luke 6:31 (NIV) says, "*Do to others as you would have them do to you.*"

When you and your spouse are communicating and spending time together, be intentional in your focus. Pay attention. Don't only hear, but truly *listen* to what your spouse is saying. I shouldn't expect my husband to pay attention to me if I am not paying attention to him. Sow into your marriage. Be willing to put *into* your marriage. Be committed first to God, then to your spouse. Be your spouse's friend. Be your spouse's confidant.

Become the spouse that can be trusted and talked to. Friendship between husbands and wives must exist for a marriage to be healthy. Learn how to be your spouse's friend, their *best* friend. Learn to listen and learn to communicate with your spouse. Learn your spouse's love language. More than likely, your spouse's love language is different than yours.

Don't only love your spouse; be their friend and learn to communicate with them in the way they need, and in the way that will minister to them. Things that mean a lot, show me love, and minister to me do not necessarily do the same for my husband. Our love languages are different. The things my husband does to and *for* me to minister to me and show me love probably isn't what I should do to and for him. We are all different.

My responsibility as my husband's wife is to honor and respect him. It is to find out what his love language is, what ministers to him, not to me, and do those things for him.

I encourage you to do the same for your spouse. Become your spouse's friend. Develop that friendship between the two of you! Walk in unity, love, and peace together. A true friend loves at all times.

> Proverbs 17:17 (TPT) says, *"A dear friend will love you no matter what, and a family sticks together through all kinds of trouble."*

> John 15:12-13 (NKJV) says, *"This is My commandment, that you love one another as I have loved you, Greater love has no one than this, than to lay down one's life for his friends."*

Can you do this for your spouse? Can you be this friend? This is unconditional love. Can you put your spouse's wants and desires above your own?

> Proverbs 18:24 (NKJV) says, *"A man who has friends must himself be friendly, but there is a friend who sticks closer than a brother."*

I truly believe friendship with our spouse is important. Study your spouse. Learn how to be the best friend your spouse could have. Enjoy your spouse and the time you spend with them. Learn how to have fun together and enjoy your journey together. Ask God to teach you how to honor your spouse and what ministers to them. Lean on God for guidance. He will direct you, speak to you, and guide you.

Let's pray:

> Father, help me to be my spouse's friend. Lead me, Lord, so I will know how to minister to them. Teach me how to listen and love the way You listen and love. Help me to be the friend my husband/wife needs. Help me to understand my spouse's needs. I desire to be _____'s (put your spouse's name here) best friend. Teach me Lord to be that person for_____.
>
> In the mighty name of Jesus!
> Amen.

Chapter 10

ONWARD AND UPWARD

In the chapters of this book, we have learned what unity means, why it is important, and why unity is so important in *marriage*. We have learned some of the biblical truths of the role of a husband, and the role of a wife. We have also learned the role of God in our marriages and how important His role is in our relationship with our spouse. We have learned about friendship in marriage. Now, it is time to take these truths, the biblical principles, and move onward and upward. It is time to apply these truths to our lives and to our marriages.

God has so much in store for you, your spouse, and your marriage. I encourage you to seek the Lord on what He wants you to do and who He wants you to be in your marriage, and for your spouse. It is time for you to step into your true identity and your God-ordained, God-planned role and position for you, your spouse, and your marriage.

Even if you feel like your marriage and relationship are perfect or it is everything you want, God is saying to you, "There is more, there is greater depths and greater levels for you."

With God, there is always more. You need to take what God has said through His Word, and through the pages of this book, and apply them to your individual lives and marriage. God wants you to have fulfilling lives and marriages more than *you* want you to have them.

Move toward unity in your marriage. There is so much *power* in unity. Why do you think the enemy, the devil, wants to keep you from walking in unity with your spouse?

This is why Jesus said, in Matthew 12:25 (NIV), *"Jesus knew their thoughts and said to them, 'Every kingdom divided against itself will be ruined, and every city or household divided against itself will not stand.'"* And, Genesis 2:24 reads, *"That is why a man leaves his father and mother and is <u>united</u> to his wife, and they become <u>one</u> flesh,"* (underlining by me).

It is important to be in unity. After all, scripture says that when you marry, you become one with your spouse. Becoming one and becoming united with your spouse is God's plan for you and your spouse.

If my spouse and I are divided, according to scripture, we cannot stand. Oh, but if we are in unity, the devil better look out, because we are a united force and he, the devil, cannot stand or prevail against us. He knows it. That's why he tries to keep you divided with your spouse. Let's not allow him to do that. Give him no place in your marriage or your life.

> Ephesians 4:26-28a (NKJV) says, "'*Be angry, and do not sin*': *do not let the sun go down on your wrath, nor give place to the devil. Let him who stole steal no longer.*"

It is time that you move onward and upward with God, and that your marriage does the same. Don't stay in the place you have been – in strife, divided, not unified or against each other, yearning for more.

Get on board with God and His plan for you and your marriage. Take your focus off of the struggles and the problems, and put you focus on your *problem solver*. Take your focus off of the negative and faults of your spouse, and put your focus on Jesus.

When we put our focus on Jesus and not our problems or our circumstances, He seems bigger than our problems and circumstances. After all, He is so much greater and bigger. If you continually keep your focus on your problems, your problems will seem so much bigger. So, *stop it*! Focus on Jesus, the author and finisher of your faith, your Problem Solver, your Redeemer, and your Deliverer!

> Hebrews 12:2 (NKJV) says, "*Looking unto Jesus, the author and finisher of our faith, who for the joy that was set before Him endured the cross, despising the shame, and has sat down at the right hand of the throne of God.*"

Colossians 3:2 (NKJV) reads, *"Set your minds on things above, not on the things on the earth."*

You and I must keep our focus on Jesus and allow Him to move in our lives and our marriages. Our focus should be on Jesus, the author and finisher of our faith. He has a plan for our lives and our marriages. If we submit to Him, yield our lives and our marriages to Him, and give Him both, He will fulfill His purposes for us.

We need to place our lives, our marriages, and our spouses in the hands of God. Forget what the past has been and focus on what is ahead.

We must lay down the way things have always been, give everything to God, yield to Him, and trust that things will be different. If I am trying to change things myself and do God's job, how can He work? I am in His way.

It is time to release ourselves, our spouses, and our marriages into His hands and allow Him to do what He wants to do. Let Him take us where He wants to. Yield your life to Him. Give Him your spouse and your marriage. Lay it all at His feet. Move out of His way and don't pick it up again… move onward and upward with Him!

He has the absolute *best* for you. You can trust God. Pray and declare what you want for your life, your marriage, and your spouse. Prophesy to your marriage. Say what God says over yourself, your spouse, and your marriage, and watch Him (God) move. You will not be disappointed.

Move onward and upward with God! There is more. Get on the journey with God. Walk with Him. Lean into Him.

Place it all at His feet, and don't pick it up again. Focus on Jesus, the author and finisher of your faith.

You and I cannot change our spouses, but God can. We must give Him room to work and move. Take your hands off of things and give everything to God. He will do it.

Let's pray:

> Father, we choose today to believe You for our own lives, for our spouses and for our marriages. We take all three and place them at Your feet. We yield our lives to You. We surrender and lay it all at Your feet. We choose to move out of Your way, let go, and let You do what You want to do. We trust You, God. Have Your way. We say to You, Father, not my will, but Yours be done! We are moving ONWARD and UPWARD with You!
>
> In the mighty name of Jesus,
> Amen!

PRAYER FOR MARRIAGES

Father, I thank You for the readers of this book and for their marriages. Father, I pray that You will give them revelation of the truth of Your Word concerning husbands, wives, unity, and marriage.

Lord, I thank You that as they read the pages of Your Word and have read the pages of this book, You will transform their lives and their marriages. Reveal Your truth to them. Father, I pray for freedom for their lives and marriages.

In Jesus's name,
Amen.

Now I encourage you to pray this prayer:

Father, I _____ (put your name here) repent for trying to change my spouse and trying to change my marriage on my own. Lord, I take _____ (say your spouse's name here) and my marriage and place them in Your hands, and I say, "Father, not my will, but Yours be done in my life, _____'s (spouse's name) life, and our marriage. Teach me Your ways, God. Help me not to lean on my own understanding. Teach me, God, how to walk in unity with _____ (put your spouse's name here). Father, I give (spouse's name) _____ and my marriage to You, and I say to You, have Your way Lord, have Your way!"

Father, thank You that You want our marriages to succeed more than we want them too. We trust You God!

> In the mighty name of Jesus, I pray,
> Amen.

OTHER BOOKS BY JENNIFER PEIKERT

Daughters of God…. Modesty Matters

Being a Proverbs 31 Woman…. What Does That Mean?

What Is a Submitted Wife….And How Do I Become One?

The Heart of a Woman

Que Es Una esposa Sometida….Y Como Convertirme En una?

www.ingramcontent.com/pod-product-compliance
Ingram Content Group UK Ltd.
Pitfield, Milton Keynes, MK11 3LW, UK
UKHW022221230426
12048UKWH00016BA/994